HORRIBLY HILARIOUS JOKE BOOK

HORRIBLE HISTORIES

READ ALL ABOUT THE NASTY BITS!

HORRIBLY HILARIOUS JOKE BOOK

SCHOLASTIC

Published in the UK by Scholastic, 2022
Euston House, 24 Eversholt Street, London, NW1 1DB
Scholastic Ireland, 89E Lagan Road, Dublin Industrial Estate, Glasnevin, Dublin, D11 HP5F

First published in the UK by Scholastic Ltd, 2009
This edition published by Scholastic Ltd, 2022

Text copyright © Terry Deary, 2009, 2019, 2022
Illustrations © Martin Brown and Philip Reeve, 2009, 2019, 2022
Additional text by Dereen Taylor

The right of Terry Deary and Martin Brown to be identified as the author and illustrator of this work has been asserted by them under the Copyright, Designs and Patents Act 1988.

ISBN 978 0702 31499 5

A CIP catalogue record for this book is available from the British Library.

Printed and bound in the UK by CPI Group (UK) Ltd, Croydon, CR0 4YY
Paper made from wood grown in sustainable forests and other controlled sources.

1 3 5 7 9 10 8 6 4 2

www.scholastic.co.uk

CONTENTS

SAVAGE
STONE AGE

A baby mammoth says to his mum:

WHY DID THE MAMMOTH HAVE A FUR COAT?
BECAUSE HE'D HAVE LOOKED SILLY IN AN ANORAK.

WHAT DO YOU CALL A CAVEMAN WHO'S BEEN BURIED SINCE THE STONE AGE?
PETE. (PEAT ... GEDDIT?)

AWFUL
EGYPTIANS

What did the Pharaoh say when he saw the pyramid? Mummy's home.

What did the mummy say when its tummy rumbled?

Did you know most of the Egyptian king Piye's people kept sheep?

He was the original shepherd's Piye.

Did you know the first mummies turned rotten because they were just wrapped in bandages?

Did you know Egyptian kings were often buried with wives, slaves and animals to stop them getting lonely in the afterlife? There are 24 horses buried near the pyramids of Kurru. When King Piye died they were killed so they could pull his chariots in the afterlife.

Did you know the Egyptians believed everybody was made up of two parts – the body and the spirit? They called the spirit 'Ka'.

Did you hear about the crooked Egyptian judge who had his ears chopped off as a punishment?
He never heard another case again.

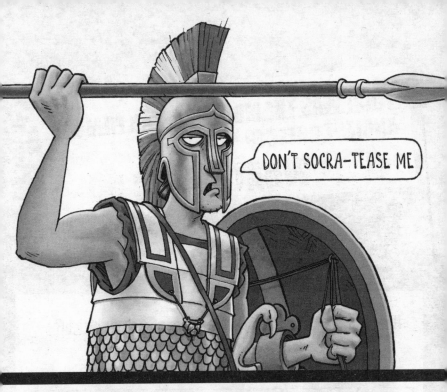

GROOVY
GREEKS

WHAT WAS THE MOST POPULAR FILM IN ANCIENT GREECE?
TROY STORY.

Have you heard the one about the famous Greek playwright?

WHAT'S THE CAPITAL OF GREECE?
G.

WHICH GREEK LEADER WAS THE BEST OF THE BUNCH?
ALEXANDER THE GRAPE.

WHY ISN'T SUNTANNING AN OLYMPIC SPORT?
BECAUSE THE BEST YOU CAN GET IS BRONZE.

ROTTEN
ROMANS

THE ROMANS CONQUERED AFRICA, THEY CONQUERED EUROPE, THEY CONQUERED BRITAIN, THEN THEY STOPPED. PROBABLY RAN OUT OF CONKERS! HEY! HEY!

GROAN

THE ROMANS DIVIDED GAUL INTO THREE PARTS — PROBABLY USED A PAIR OF CAESARS! HEE! HEE!

I WISH SOMEONE WOULD DIVIDE HER IN THREE PARTS

WHAT DID CAESAR SAY AFTER BRUTUS STABBED HIM?
OUCH!

WHERE DID CAESAR KEEP HIS ARMIES?
UP HIS SLEEVIES.

WHEN DID CAESAR REIGN?
I DIDN'T KNOW HE REIGNED.
OF COURSE HE DID, THAT'S WHY THEY HAILED HIM.

SMASHING
SAXONS

WHY WAS KING ALFRED CALLED 'THE GREAT'?
BECAUSE ALFRED THE BLOOMING MARVELLOUS WOULD HAVE SOUNDED SILLY.

WHAT DO ALFRED THE GREAT AND WINNIE THE POOH HAVE IN COMMON?
THEIR MIDDLE NAME.

WHICH ENGLISH KING INVENTED THE FIREPLACE?
ALFRED THE GRATE.

CUT-THROAT CELTS

Did you know the Celts believed death could be explained by the four elements – water, air, earth or fire?

Did you know the Celts believed that pigs were very wise, so they listened to what pigs had to say?

Did you know the Celts had a law against damaging trees?

VICIOUS
VIKINGS

WHEN WAS THE BEST TIME FOR VIKINGS TO ATTACK?
DURING A PLUNDER STORM.

WHERE DID THE VIKINGS LAND WHEN THEY CAME TO ENGLAND?
ON THEIR FEET.

MEASLY
MIDDLE AGES

What did the sick knight say?
I feel like black death warmed up.

Did you know William the Conqueror's son Richard came to a painful end? He collided with a tree when he was riding his horse.

FELLED BY A STROKE FROM AN OAK?

NAH. IT WAS A BASH FROM AN ASH

WHAT WAS THE MIDDLE AGES FAMOUS FOR?
ITS KNIGHT LIFE.

WHAT'S ANOTHER TERM FOR MIDDLE AGES?
KNIGHT TIME.

WHERE WAS THE MAGNA CARTA SIGNED?
AT THE BOTTOM.

In medieval times toilets were little rooms that jutted out from the walls of a castle. Human waste dropped straight down into the moat below.

WHAT DO YOU PUT ON THE GRAVESTONE OF A KNIGHT IN SHINING ARMOUR?
'RUST IN PEACE'.

WHAT DID THE DRAGON SAY WHEN HE SAW THE KNIGHT IN SHINING ARMOUR?
I HATE TINNED FOOD.

IT'S A HANDY WALL-HOLE!

WHY DID THE KNIGHT PULL OUT OF THE ARCHERY CONTEST?
HE FOUND IT AN ARROWING EXPERIENCE.

YOU CAN'T GET THE BUILDERS THESE DAYS.

LADY: WE HAD BOAR FOR DINNER LAST NIGHT.
KNIGHT: WILD?
LADY: WELL, LET'S JUST SAY HE WASN'T TOO PLEASED.

One evening a knight was riding to the rescue of a beautiful maiden – as knights do – when he ran into a terrible storm. Lightning flashed and thunder rolled – lightning rolled and thunder flashed. A bolt of lightning flashed down and hit the knight's horse, which collapsed and died.

The knight staggered into a miserable little village and hammered on the door of the inn. The landlord answered the knock and the knight threw himself, dripping wet, through the door.

"Good grief, sire! I wouldn't let a dog go out on a night like this! Come in! Come in!"

The knight gasped, "Landlord! Landlord! Give me your finest horse, whatever it costs!"

"Sorry, sire, we're right out of horses!"

"Then give me a pony, or a donkey!"

Sorry, sire, no ponies, no donkeys, not even a ponkey!"

"Then what have you got?" the knight begged.

"Just a giant Irish hunting dog, sire. Here it is, by the fire. Good boy, Paddy!" the landlord said and clicked his fingers. The dog rose to its feet. It was huge. Almost as big as a pony and strong enough to take the knight. The trouble is it had been out in the rain and its mangy coat was steaming and stinking. It limped over to the door.

The smell of the dog almost made the knight throw up. But he put the saddle on the dog and threw his leg over the animal's scabby back. The animal swayed and limped towards the door, panting with breath so foul it almost made the knight faint.

The landlord opened the door and looked out into the lashing rain and flashing thunder. He closed the door and shook his head. "Sorry, sire, but I wouldn't let a knight go out on a dog like this!"

Did you know the Aztecs thought the body of a woman who had died in childbirth had magical powers? Warriors cut off parts of the body and fastened them to their shields to protect them in battle.

WHY DID CHRISTOPHER COLUMBUS SAIL TO AMERICA?
IT WAS TOO FAR TO SWIM.

HOW DO YOU MAKE A MEXICAN CHILLI?
TAKE HIM TO THE NORTH POLE.

INCREDIBLE
INCAS

Did you know the Incas thought the first people came from a hole in the ground?

Did you know the Incas didn't use money? They exchanged their work for what they wanted. Might not work at school though...

TERRIBLE
TUDORS

WHY COULDN'T HENRY VIII BREATHE?
HE NEEDED AN HEIR.

WHICH ONE OF HENRY VIII'S WIVES LIKED PLAYING SKITTLES?
ANNE BOWLING

SPLAT

SPLAT

SPLAT

SPLAT

SPLAT

Henry VIII

Henry VIII was as fat as a boar
Had six wives and still wanted more.
Anne and Kate said, 'By heck!
He's a pain in the neck!'
As their heads landed smack on the floor.

Mary I

Bloody Mary, they say, was quite mad.
And the nastiest taste that she had
Was for Protestant burning
Seems she had a yearning
To kill even more than her dad.

Elizabeth I

A truly great queen was old Lizzie,
She went charging around being busy.
She thought herself beaut,
But her teeth looked like soot
And her hair it was all red and frizzy.

WHAT DID THE EXECUTIONER SAY TO THE PRISONER?
TIME TO HEAD OFF.

WHY WAS THE GHOST OF ANNE BOLEYN ALWAYS RUNNING?
SHE WANTED TO GET A-HEAD.

WHEN DID HENRY VIII DIE?
A FEW DAYS BEFORE THEY BURIED HIM.

WHICH QUEEN WAS THE BEST AT FOOTBALL?
ANNE – BECAUSE SHE GOT THE BOLEYN.
(BALL-IN ... GEDDIT?)

WHAT HAPPENED WHEN ELIZABETH I BURPED?
SHE ISSUED A ROYAL PARDON.

TUDOR MAN: DO YOU WANT TO COME TO A PARTY TONIGHT?
TUDOR WOMAN: NO, I'M GOING TO SEE ROMEO AND JULIET.
TUDOR MAN: WELL BRING THEM ALONG WITH YOU.

WHICH QUEEN OF ENGLAND HAD THE LARGEST CROWN?
THE ONE WITH THE LARGEST HEAD.

Why did Henry VIII have so many wives? He liked to chop and change.

SLIMY
STUARTS

PUTRID
PIRATES

What do pirates eat for tea?

What do you say to a pirate prisoner who is being punished by having iron bolts jammed in his mouth?

Why did the pirate need some soap?
To wash himself ashore.

Why did the one-handed pirate cross the road?
He wanted to get to the second-hand shop.

GORGEOUS
GEORGIANS

Did you know that Georgian women wore real flowers, fruit and vegetables on their heads?

WHY DIDN'T NAPOLEON LIKE TO GO OUT IF IT WAS WINDY? IN CASE HE GOT BLOWN APART. (BONAPARTE ... GEDDIT? NO? OH, NEVER MIND!)

VILE
VICTORIANS

Did you know that in Victorian times, if you were caught chopping down someone else's tree you could be hanged?

Did you know a 'bogie' was another name for a Victorian policeman?

Did you know that when Victorian prisons were full, criminals were sent to 'hulks'? These were smelly, rat-infested old ships that were too ancient and rotten to sail.

What did the Victorian child imprisoned for stealing a pair of trousers say?

What did the Victorian child imprisoned for pinching apples say?

FRIGHTFUL
FIRST WORLD
WAR

There was a young Boche at Bazentin
Who liked the first trench that he went in.
But a 15 inch 'dud'
Sent him flat in the mud
And he found that his helmet was bent in.

There were lots of lies flying around during the First World War. The Brits didn't even trust their allies, the French.

I'VE HEARD THAT THE FRENCH ARE CHARGING US RENT TO LIVE IN THE TRENCHES IN FRANCE! WE'LL BE BLED OF EVERY PENNY

SO IT'S A SORT OF BLED AND BREAKFAST, HUH?

The Brits were sure the Germans were desperate for materials and especially fat...

SAYS HERE THE GERMANS ARE TAKING THE FAT OFF THEIR CORPSES TO MAKE EXPLOSIVES

THEY'D LOVE TO MEET YOU THEN

The Brits were also sure that Germany was running short of fighting men...

THEY'RE NOT GERMAN SOLDIERS YOU SEE IN THE TRENCHES. THEY ARE DUMMIES STUFFED WITH STRAW, AND CORPSES

THEY'LL BE DEAD SHOTS THEN!

WWI soldiers in the trenches enjoyed a joke about the senior officers who were miles behind the lines when the shooting started. One popular cartoon was this one...

General (addressing the men before practising an attack in the training camp): 'I want you to understand that there are three essential differences between a rehearsal and the real thing. First, the absence of the enemy, now (turning to the Sergeant Major), what is the second difference?
Sergeant Major: 'The absence of a general, sir.'

Did you know during a battle in Poland, German soldiers were trampled to death by a herd of European bison?

Did you know female factory workers used TNT explosive powder to give their hair a chestnut colour. But a red-head could become red-hot if you struck a match near her hair!

WOEFUL
SECOND WORLD
WAR

Officer, a filthy Nazi spy has been here. How can you tell?

BECAUSE HE WENT TO THE TOILET BUT HE DIDN'T PULL THE CHAIN

One of the ways people survived the horrors of concentration camps was humour. A popular Jewish joke about the German guards in the camps went like this...

I HAVE A GLASS EYE. IF YOU CAN TELL ME WHICH EYE IS THE GLASS ONE THEN I'LL LET YOU LIVE

IT'S YOUR RIGHT EYE

AMAZING! HOW DID YOU KNOW?

THAT'S THE EYE WITH A KIND EXPRESSION IN IT

During WWII British children were evacuated to homes in the countryside. One grand country lady complained to a rough evacuee's mother...

BUT HE DROPPED HIS TROUSERS AND HAD A POO IN THE MIDDLE OF THE CARPET

The mother grabbed the child, smacked him and reminded him...

BIFF

YOU DIRTY THING, MESSING UP THE LADY'S CARPET. WHY DIDN'T YOU DO IT IN THE CORNER LIKE I SHOWED YOU. EH?

and finally...

WHY DID THE PUPIL MISS HIS HISTORY EXAM?
HE HAD THE WRONG DATE.

SIR, SIR, I HAVEN'T DONE MY HISTORY HOMEWORK.
DON'T WORRY ABOUT IT. IT'S ALL IN THE PAST.

WHY DID THE HISTORY TEACHER NOT GO TO THE PARTY?
HE COULDN'T FIND A DATE.

TEACHER: WHY IS YOUR HISTORY HOMEWORK IN YOUR FATHER'S WRITING?
PUPIL: BECAUSE I USED HIS PEN.

WHY IS HISTORY THE FRUITIEST SUBJECT AT SCHOOL?
IT'S FULL OF DATES.

COLLECT THEM ALL!

RAGGED STAR

❖

Gerry McDonnell

❖

Belfast
LAPWING

First Published by Lapwing Publications
c/o 1, Ballysillan Drive
Belfast BT14 8HQ
lapwing.poetry@ntlworld.com
http://www.freewebs.com/lapwingpoetry/

Since before 1632
The Greig sept of the MacGregor Clan
Has been printing and binding books

All Lapwing Publications are
Printed and Hand-bound in Belfast
Set in Aldine 721 BT at the Winepress

ISBN 978-1-907276-83-5

ii